Level 3
High Beginner

Palace of Bean

tiger**aspect**
PRODUCTIONS
an endemol company

Popcorn
ELT
Readers

Meet ...
the people in

mr Bean™

Mr Bean

This is Mr Bean. He lives in London. He likes the Queen.

The Queen

This is the Queen. She lives in London too.

Teddy

This is Teddy. He's Mr Bean's best friend.

Brad

This is Brad. He's from the USA, but he's in London for a week.

Mrs Wicket

This is Mrs Wicket. She isn't very nice. Mr Bean lives in some rooms in her house.

Mary

This is Mary. She's Mrs Wicket's friend.

Before you read ...

In this story, people give someone a lot of money. Who are they going to give the money to?

New Words

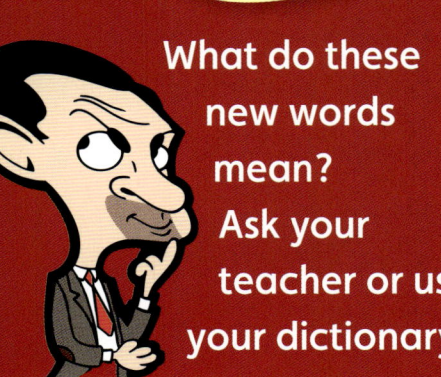

What do these new words mean?
Ask your teacher or use your dictionary.

paint

Jem has some **paint**. She is **painting** her room.

curtain

These **curtains** are blue.

palace

This is a palace.

package

It's a **package** for me!

pattern

I like this **pattern.**

remember

Hello …

She didn't **remember** his name.

take photos

I like **taking photos**.

video

Let's watch a **video**!

wall

This is a **wall**.

Verbs

Present	Past
fall	fell
sit	sat

THE WORLD OF BEAN

We wanted to know more about Mr Bean! So we went to his house to ask some questions ...

Q Hello, Mr Bean. What's your first name?

A I don't know. Maybe it's 'Mr'.

Q Oh! Is there a Mrs Bean?

A Before I go to bed, I read the phone book. There are about thirty Mrs Beans in there.

This is my green Mini.

I see ... Who's your best friend?

 I've got two best friends – Teddy and my green Mini.

 What do you like doing in your free time?

 I like staying at home.

 What do you like doing when you go out?

 I like coming home again. Can you go now? I have to make dinner for Teddy!

– Oh, OK!
Thank you, Mr Bean!

What do these words mean? Find out.
phone book   free time

The Palace of Bean

It was Monday morning. There were two packages at Mr Bean's house.

Great! Two packages for me!

And what's this?

Oh! It's for Mrs Wicket.

Mrs Wicket
112 Arbour Road,
London
N2 3KM

Here you are, Mrs Wicket. Now I can open my packages!

Oh good! Something for me!

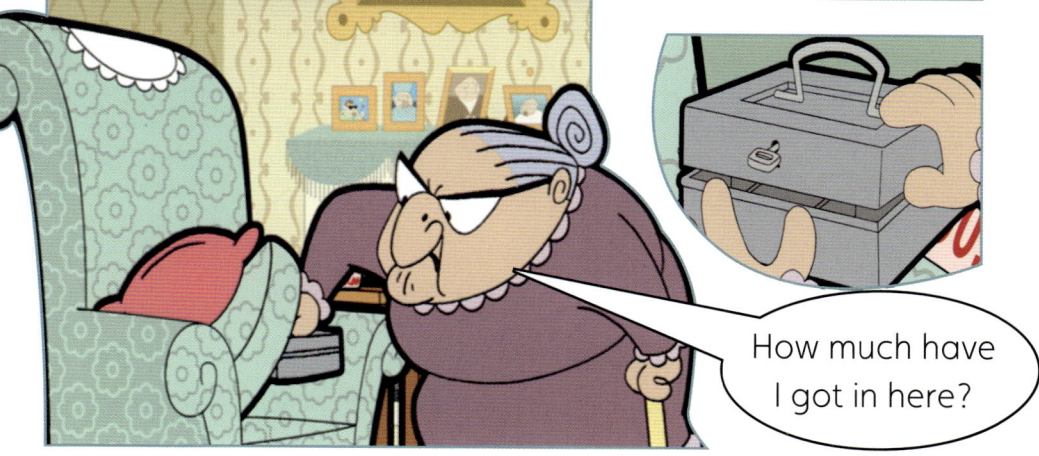

Mr Bean went into his room.

Teddy was on his chair.

Look, Teddy. The packages are here!

Is this my picture of the Queen?

Yes, it is. Good morning, Your Majesty *.

And is this my video of the Queen?

Yes, it is. This is very exciting!

* When you speak to the Queen, you say 'Your Majesty'.

Mr Bean sat down.

Let's watch the video now, Teddy!

The video started.

Today the Queen is looking at new colours for her walls …

There's this, Your Majesty.

No, I don't like that. What do you think, Teddy?

No. It's horrible.

A lot of people like this, Your Majesty.

Yes, I like it too.

Oh, Your Majesty! That's very nice!

11

Mr Bean went to the garden to look for something.

Not that!

Not that!

He looked and looked.

Not that!
Or that! Or that!

This is it!
Green paint!

But now Mr Bean had a problem.

Wait! I can't remember the pattern. I need to watch the video again.

The TV is under here ... but where?

Oh good! There it is!

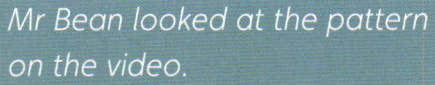
Mr Bean looked at the pattern on the video.

How can I make that green pattern?

Oh, I know! Teddy, come with me!

Are you OK there, Teddy?

Mr Bean put Teddy into the paint.

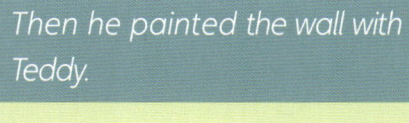
Then he painted the wall with Teddy.

That's very good, Teddy!

Do you like it, Your Majesty?

Me too!

Mr Bean looked at the picture of the Queen again. She had red curtains.

I want red curtains too!

My old curtains are going to be beautiful soon.

Then he did some more work on the room.

Now I need something on my head ... I know!

This is great!

Mr Bean was very happy. The room was beautiful.

Brad came down the road and stopped at Mr Bean's house.

Look at that! The Queen's palace!

Mrs Wicket wanted Mary's money.

How much is in your bag?

But it's *my* money! I don't want to give it to you.

Give it to me, Mary! **NOW!**

Brad came into the room.

Hi!

That's a great photo! Thank you.

Brad went into Mr Bean's room.

The Queen's bedroom! This is exciting!

Mr Bean was in his chair.

What are you doing here?

Can I take some photos?

Yes ... that's OK.

That's a great bed. The Queen likes red!

Your room wasn't this colour before. What did you do to it, Mr Bean?

18

I ... I ...

I can't hear you, Mr Bean!

Thank you for your time, everyone. Here's something for you. Bye!

Brad went out. Mrs Wicket didn't see his £5 on the table.

£5

What's that in your hand?

I'm going to have that, Mr Bean.

Now Mrs Wicket was the Queen!

Suddenly Mrs Wicket saw something.

Oh, look! What's that on the table?

£5! The American gave us £5.

Next day more people came.

They all had money.

They gave the money to Mary. They wanted to see the Queen's palace.

Thank you very much!

Everyone liked the room.

They loved taking photos of Mrs Wicket.

Mrs Wicket loved sitting in Mr Bean's chair, but Mr Bean wasn't happy.

Up and down!
Up and down!

It's hot in here.
Move it faster,
Mr Bean!

But my arms
are tired!

When the people went home, it was very late.

There was a lot of money.

How much have we got?

That's a good day's work. Here's £5 for you, Mary.

Thank you!

And how much for me?

That night, Mr Bean watched more of his video.

The yellow and green is OK, but have you got anything nicer?

What?!

OK, Your Majesty.

Yes! This is beautiful. I want this.

No! What am I going to do?

Mr Bean went into the garden.

Here it is!

Next day …

Good morning, everyone!

Oh! It's horrible!

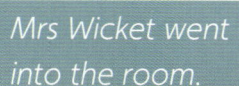

Mrs Wicket went into the room.

Good morning, Mrs Wicket.

Oh no! Where are the yellow and green walls, Mr Bean? Where are the red curtains?

I don't want them. But I want *this*, Mrs Wicket.

And we want our money.

That's better. It's quiet now. And brown is a very nice colour.

Mrs Wicket wasn't happy.

Don't go! Please don't go!

CRASH!

Oh no!

THE END

Real World

The British Queen

Mr Bean likes the Queen. Let's find out more about her.

The Queen

Who is she?

Queen Elizabeth II (Elizabeth the Second). She was born in 1926 and became Queen in 1952.

She made her first speech – to the children of the UK – when she was 14 years old.

Where does she live?

At Buckingham Palace in London. The palace is 300 years old. If there is a flag on the palace, the Queen is at home.

The Queen also has a palace in Scotland – Holyroodhouse – and a lot more houses too.

The Queen at 14

Wow! Is she very rich?

Yes, she is, but she isn't the richest woman in Britain. J.K. Rowling, the writer of Harry Potter, is richer than the Queen.

Has she got any children?

Yes, she has got four children. The oldest is Prince Charles.

When the Queen dies, Charles becomes King. Charles' oldest child is Prince William.

Buckingham Palace

Prince William

Do you know any more places with a king or queen?

What do these words mean? Find out.

was born
become / became (past)
speech   die   king

After you read

1 Match the questions and answers.

a) Who needs money?   **i)** Teddy

b) Who likes the Queen?   **ii)** Mrs Wicket

c) Who is on Mr Bean's video? **iii)** Mr Bean

d) Who likes taking photos? **iv)** The Queen

e) Who does Mr Bean put in   **v)** Brad.

   the green paint?

2 True ✓ or False ✗? Write in the box.

a) Mr Bean found some green paint. ☑

b) Brad went to the Queen's palace. ☐

c) People gave a lot of money to Mary. ☐

d) Mrs Wicket gave a lot of money to Mr Bean. ☐

e) At the end of the story, the Queen had green
and yellow walls. ☐

f) Everybody liked Mr Bean's room with brown walls. ☐

Where's the popcorn?
Look in your book.
Can you find it?

Puzzle time!

1 Do the puzzle and answer the question.

| | 1 | P | A | I | N | T |
| | | | | | | |

Where's the Queen?   At the _ _ _ _ _ _

2 Who or what is this?

a .... Brad

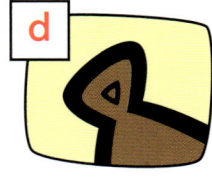
d ....

b ....

e ....

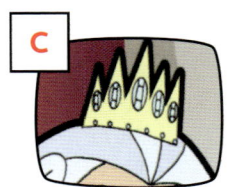
c ....

f ....

3 What's in picture A but not in picture B? Circle six things and write.

a) ...paint.........   b) ....   c) ....

d) ....   e) ....   f) ....

4 Whose packages are these? Read and write the names.

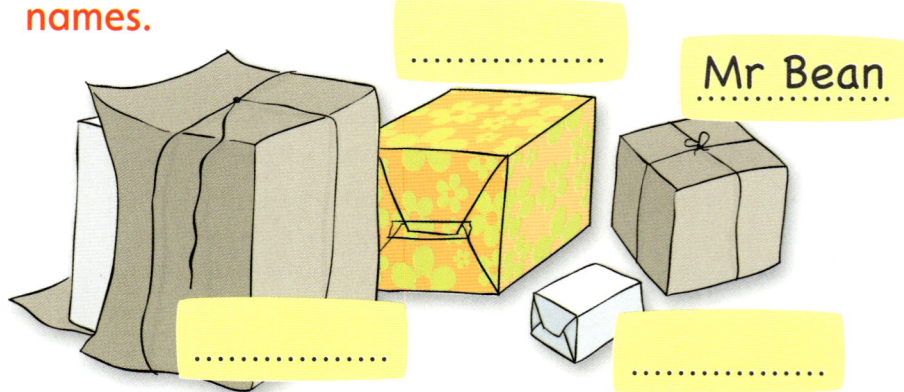

Mr Bean

Mr Bean's package isn't big and it isn't small.

Mary's package has a pattern on it.

Teddy's package is the smallest.

Mrs Wicket's package is open.

Imagine ...

**Work in groups. Mime a scene from the story.
Can your friends guess what you are doing?**

Are you in a car?

No, I'm not.

Are you watching a video?

Yes, I am!

Chant

1 🔊 **Listen and read.**

It's Mr Bean!

Who is this?
It's Mr Bean!
He paints his room
So it's yellow and green.
His curtains, bed and chair are red.
'This is the Queen's room,' people said.
They want to take photos.
They give him money.
But now the room's brown.
That's not funny!

2 🔊 **Say the chant.**